Deck of Choices

31 Essential Tips for Leaders

By

Phillis Clements

Deck of Choices – 31 Essential Tips for Leaders

Copyright © 2014 Phillis Clements

All Rights Reserved.

Published in the United States

Cover photo from MorgueFile

ISBN-13: 978-1517630317
ISBN-10: 1517630312

1. Leadership Development
2. Motivational - Inspirational

Foreword

A large part of my philosophy about life is based on the belief that each of us has the ability to make choices. In every situation we have a choice. No matter how positive or negative the choice may be, there is a choice to be made and it is ours to own. This does not dismiss the fact that there are things outside of our control that will impact the choices we make. How we respond to those things we do not control starts with a choice. This is especially true for leaders. As such, we must be more conscious about how our choices impact our behaviors as they will inevitably influence the choices being made by those who follow us.

I have given you a month's worth of choices to become familiar with or refresh, along with an action step for each to assist you with developing the habit of applying these leadership attributes as you interact with others. It is my hope that this book will help you to be a more effective leader.

**Always remember that
your CHOICE matters!**

Accountability

Today's Lesson in Choice:

Leaders are accountable for their actions and the actions of those they are responsible for. Effective leaders don't make excuses; they take responsibility when things go wrong, and praise those who did the work when things go right.

I will take ownership and share recognition with others for successes achieved.

Attitude

Today's Lesson in Choice:

Attitude influences our choices, decisions and actions. Understand that attitudes are formed as a result of experience, but can also be learned. How you feel, think or behave towards others can have a ripple effect.

I will be clear about why I have the attitudes I do and change those that are in conflict with my values and beliefs.

———————

Authentic

Today's Lesson in Choice:

A real leader genuinely cares about others. They say what they mean and mean what they say.

I will be sincere in my dealings with others.

———————————

Belief

Today's Lesson in Choice:

Belief is about having conviction and confidence in the existence of something or someone. Trust and faith in something we believe in is not about everything turning out alright. it's about being okay no matter how everything turns out. I will choose what I believe.

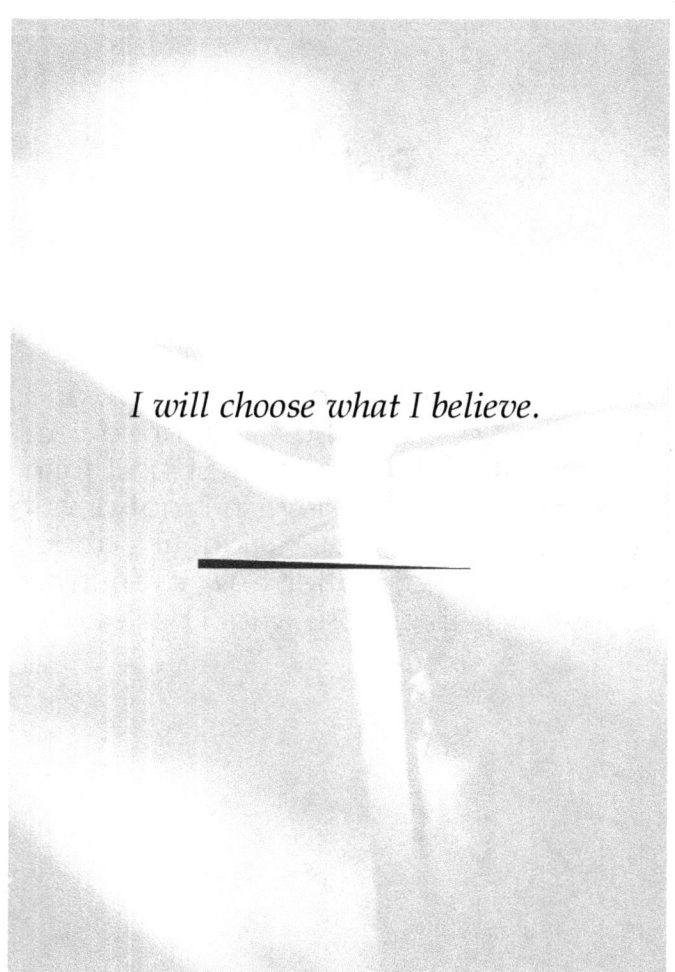

I will choose what I believe.

Change

Today's Lesson in Choice:

Change is the inevitable transformation that takes place with the passage of time. An alteration, modification, variation and transition from what was to what is and will be.

I will celebrate the change that takes place with each new day.

Choice

Today's Lesson in Choice:

Choice is about options that lead to decisions. Choice can create transformation and is the one power that cannot be taken away. It is magical. You can give it away or keep it.

I will cultivate my choices, protect them, and exercise them as often as possible.

———

Communication

Today's Lesson in Choice:

A leader must be able to effectively share knowledge and ideas in a way that inspires others to act. Transparency about decisions and lessons learned helps to build trust.

I will be transparent and communicate effectively and often.

Courage

Today's Lesson in Choice:

Some would say courage is the ability to act in the face of fear; others say it means to have the confidence to do the right thing no matter the consequence. Both are correct.

As a leader, I will demonstrate courage.

━━━━━━━━━━

Development

Today's Lesson in Choice:

Recognizing potential and developing the skills of folks through targeted learning opportunities demonstrates ones commitment to cultivating talent.

I will create development plans that address individual needs and meet organizational goals.

Empowerment

Today's Lesson in Choice:

It is only through the sharing of a vision and the delegation of au-hority that others feel empowered to act. As leaders, we must create an environment for others to be creative, learn, grow and exercise sound judgment.

I will enable the empowerment of others.

———————————

Faith

Today's Lesson in Choice:

Faith means something different to each of us. It is an overwhelming belief and trust in something greater than ourselves. You can develop the strength you need by opening your mind and your heart to that which your soul knows to be the truth.

I will have faith and trust in the truth.

———

Flexibility

Today's Lesson in Choice:

Being open to change and new information is an indicator of flexibility.

I will adapt to changing conditions or unexpected obstacles and new information received.

Growth

Today's Lesson in Choice:

Growth is the process of development we see with the passage of time. This evolution is a gradual change and with the right nourishment will result in a metamorphosis. Having a growth mindset reinforces the path to evolutionary transformation.

I will be open to learning, to progress and change.

———————

Humility

Today's Lesson in Choice:

To be meek or modest in manner is a quality that will serve us well in life and business. Humility is a product of feeling. Not being prideful or arrogant takes conscious thought.

I will be humble.

Humor

Today's Lesson in Choice:

A positive sense of humor is infectious and promotes a more productive environment.

I will laugh at the good all around, and even myself, but never at the expense of others.

Innovative

Today's Lesson in Choice:

An innovative leader can bring together folks in a way that effectively leverages their differences and passion to achieve goals using new ideas.

I will be a change agent who is not afraid to challenge conventional approaches.

Inspiration

Today's Lesson in Choice:

Inspiration comes from within. It is driven by divine guidance which is displayed by influence to our mind and soul. Inspiration when influenced by outside forces becomes motivation and causes you to act.

I will actively seek inspiration and use it to create a positive existence for others.

Integrity

Today's Lesson in Choice:

Fairness, ethics and good intentions resonate with us because we believe in moral rightness. To have honor is to have integrity in one's beliefs and actions.

*I will act with integrity,
impartiality and reasonableness.*

Invest

Today's Lesson in Choice:

Building relationships and cultivating talent is essential to creating an environment of organizational effectiveness. A leader must be willing to share wisdom, leverage talent and reward performance.

I will consistently invest in myself and others.

Listening

Today's Lesson in Choice:

To listen for understanding rather than for judgment is the sign of true a leader.

I will be silent so that I can receive the whole message.

———————

Mindset

Today's Lesson in Choice:

Mindset is an attitude we have about how we approach situations. The attitudes we have are often based on a set of values and beliefs about what we feel can be accomplished. The great thing is that we can change our attitudes whenever we want. All it takes is for you to make a choice to do so.

Today I choose to be open to new ways of thinking.

Partnering

Today's Lesson in Choice:

Partnering requires one to develop networks and build alliances while collaborating across bourdaries to build strategic connections to achieve common goals.

*I will develop strong relationships
and resolve issues with others to
ensure future partnerships.*

Patience

Today's Lesson in Choice:

There are times when we have difficulty with self-control. It takes fortitude and endurance to face situations that are painful or annoying. Being patient means to keep ones composure or show tolerance.

Today I will practice patience.

———————————

Positivity

Today's Lesson in Choice:

Positivity is about having a tendency toward emphasizing what is good. To see the best and expect the best in all things is a quality that must be nurtured. Remember that the universe will return that which is put forth.

To receive positivity I will project positivity.

———————————

Problem-Solving

Today's Lesson in Choice:

Effective leaders are great problem solvers. They are open-minded, transparent communicators, and collaborative strategists. By weighing the relevance and accuracy of information, leaders generate and evaluate alternative solutions; before making recommendations.

I will leverage the knowledge and strength of others to solve problems.

Respect

Today's Lesson in Choice:

It is inevitable that we will interact with others during our lifetime. This being so, we must learn to show respect in order to forge relationships that result in reciprocal consideration.

As I develop rapport with others I will show regard for them while demonstrating my commitment to the value I bring.

Teachable

Today's Lesson in Choice:

No one can know everythirg. A leader is constantly learning and willingly receives feedback in order to be better.

I will be open to being taught.

———————————

Teambuilding

Today's Lesson in Choice:

Including others in the decision-making process of developing a mission and goals while properly defining roles and responsibilities will inspire and foster team commitment.

I will facilitate cooperation and motivate team members to accomplish group goals.

Transformational

Today's Lesson in Choice:

A transformational leader inspires others to change their perceptions, expectations and work toward a common goal.

*I will communicate a clear vision,
promote innovation and provide
encouragement and support consistently.*

Trust

Today's Lesson in Choice:

Having confidence in the truth and belief in the certainty of another is what trust is all about. Trust is hope and faith. To do something without fear of corsequences is to trust in that which is guaranteed to be.

I will create an environment of trust.

Vision

Today's Lesson in Choice:

Having a vision means being able to clearly describe a mental picture of the future and leveraging the belief that you can make it a reality.

I will be a catalyst for change and enlist others to achieve it.

About Phillis Clements

Phillis Clements positively inspires audiences as a sought after speaker, certified life coach, author, and successful entrepreneur. Through her company Sunshine Solutions she is dedicated to helping others achieve success in life and business.

Learn how to develop the habit of living an empowered life through the power of CHOICE.

Book publishing
- *Fiction/Non-fiction*
- *Company handbooks*
- *Promotional booklets*
- *Workbooks*

Contact Phillis to speak, for coaching and training at reachme@phillisinspires.com

Visit www.sunshinesolutions7.com today!